Make Money Online Within a Week

BY

MIKE TRISTAN

Why You Should Read This Book

This book will help you find your own way of making money online, and helps you to do it properly. The Internet enables everyone to start making money online within a week. It offers numerous perks ranging from the flexibility of time, nature of work and workspace.

Flexible timing and freedom to work are making online jobs really famous. Online work doesn't demand fixed timing. You will get independence and flexibility to work. You can work as a freelance counselor, blogger or writer. The best part of the online job is that you can manage it with your permanent job. There is no need to worry about tricky interviews. Just select your own job as per your interest and start working.

For those who like to write and publish his or her very own eBook this book includes a step-by-step tutorial on what to do exactly, and also in the most efficient way. After reading this book you will be able to write your own eBook within a week!

Table of Contents

WHY YOU SHOULD READ THIS BOOK	2
TABLE OF CONTENTS	3
INDEPENDENCE	5
THE SKY IS THE LIMIT	6
QUIT YOUR JOB	7
3 FASTEST WAYS TO MAKE MONEY WITHOUT INVESTING MONEY	8
KINDLE EBOOK PUBLISHING	9
SELLING YOUR OWN PRODUCTS ONLINE	11
FREELANCE WRITING	12
3 BEST WAYS TO MAKE MORE MONEY WITH INVESTING MONEY	13
ONLINE BUSINESS	14
YOUTUBE CHANNEL	15
AFFILIATE MARKETING	16

7 STEPS TO WRITE YOUR VERY OWN EBOOK FOR KINDLE 17

ONE LAST THING... 25

Independence

Online jobs offer maximum independence because there is no need to be punctual like a regular office job. Numerous companies have very hard rules for the punctuality and attendance of their employees. If you are lazy enough to find it difficult to come out of bed, you will possibly get fired from your job within a few days. On the other hand, online jobs allow you to work flexibly as per your convenience. You will become your boss and get a good amount of time to spend with your family and do what is really important. Moreover, online jobs will add an additional income stream to your life and increase your financial independence. It could even be your primary income stream.

Depending on the traffic and niche, there is a great potential to carve out an online brand. You can generate good revenue via online jobs. You can sell your own products through affiliate shops, drop ship programs or start your online business store. Women can generate a good income by working online without leaving their children at home. If you want to create a steady income stream, an online job will be a good choice for you. You can fill survey forms, write articles, recipe books or offer development services as per your expertise.

The Sky Is the Limit

While making money online, you have numerous options to ear ranging from content writing, filling surveys, transcribing and numerous others. Some jobs require no particular degree, but the others may need particular qualification. Everyone can make money online without particular qualifications. There will be huge opportunities at your doorstep. There is no need to become an expert in the field because you can start working as a beginner. With the passage of time, you can become an expert in your field.

If you are good in writing, feel free to draft an e-book on different topics and sell this book online. You can start your own blog on a particular niche or design templates for a website. You can start an online store to sell products. There is no need to meet the similar people or hear the firing threats from the boss. Online jobs allow you to work from home and connect with people of different cultures. You will become your own boss and choose your salary. You can increase comfort in your life by increasing your income. It will be a good way to increase your monthly savings. It will be good to accumulate extra money in a bank account for the future expenses and living.

Quit Your Job

It is a reality that people, who make money through online jobs, stay away from stress and numerous health problems. Almost 90 percent of people who are doing office job go through numerous stress-related health problems. During office jobs, there are high chances to catch infections, fever or flu. If you want to avoid medical expenses, it will be good to make online money and quit your job. With online jobs, your stress level will gradually decrease. You will be able to give your 100 percent to your job. Instead of sitting in the office for a long time, you can easily work at the home and control your working environment.

You can work on a laptop and sit in garden or lawn with a cup of coffee or tea. The refresh surroundings can make you feel relaxed and comfortable. It will be a good way to become efficient and productive. Working in a relaxed environment can increase your productivity. In the first step, you have to find out your actual potential and start working part-time. Once you are satisfied with your job, you can quit your office job. It will help you to save transportation expenses. You will be able to save money at a faster rate. Online jobs offer a great opportunity to students and housewives to earn money during free hours.

3 Fastest ways to make money without investing money

There are hundreds of ways to earn online money without any investment, but it is essential to find legit methods. Keep it in mind that along with legitimate online earning sources, there are numerous scam sources. You have to stay away from frauds on the internet because these people always try to steal your money. It doesn't mean to avoid online jobs because there are numerous sources to earn money. Just find out online jobs as per your interest and start earning money. If you have good writing skills or have something to sell online, you can get the advantage of these business opportunities. Find 3 fastest ways to make money without investing money.

Kindle eBook Publishing

Publishing eBooks for Kindle reader is really profitable. Amazon allows everyone write an eBook, make its cover, format it and become a self-published author. Publishing on an Amazon store is not difficult. You have to write a book with useful content and simply upload this book on the servers of Amazon for review.

If you are using MS Word, you can simply upload a word document.

If you want to earn money from an eBook, you have to write real content and proofread it. You can't move onward without professional editing. You can publish a book including a cover and the content. Once the folks at Amazon review your eBook, it will automatically go live in the store and you will become a published author. Lots of independent writers are getting attracted toward Kindle publishing. If you want to earn a good amount of money, you can make real money by selling Kindle books.

Numerous authors in the Amazon Kindle publishing are famous for their tremendous success, such as Huge Howey and Steve Scott. These authors are famous for their books and transparent earnings. Numerous published authors on Kindle are earning over $3,000 a month. To make online money, sign up for Kindle Direct Publishing (KDP) account. With KDP account, you can add new books to your particular bookshelf within a few minutes. You have to fill the title of the book, the name of author, description, upload one book cover and upload the e-book file. Choose the price of your book and finally hit publish. KDP takes usually no more than24 hours to review your book and make it available for sale on Amazon Kindle all over the world.

Amazon does whole marketing and selling for you and pays you 70% royalty for each sale within a specific price range within $2,99-$9,99. Otherwise you get 30% royalty. If you want to earn money, you have to find a good and profitable idea or niche for the book. You will need a title for your eBook and design a cover for this book. You can easily create a cover with the help of Amazon when you upload your book. You can personally write a book or simply hire writers for writing. There are numerous methods to market your book, such as optimize a book for sales or get reviews. You can choose topics like self-development, cooking, or dieting to write a book for. It will be a good way to earn money.

Selling your own products online

If you have good products to sell in the market, you can design an online store to start selling them online. Before starting an online sale, make sure to test the response of people about your products. If you see similar products in the market, check the reviews of people about these products. It will give you an idea of your market. Make a unique page for every product. It is essential to write a unique description for every product instead of copying the manufacturer's copy.

User reviews will become unique content for your products and help you to persuade other people to make purchases. Your shopping cart system should be simple enough. An easy payment system can increase shopping opportunities. Almost 3 weeks after the transaction, send an email to your customer and ask him/her to leave a honest review on your product. If a product is out of stock, ask for details of customers and call your customers when the stock is available.

Monitor the shopping trends and see what products people are searching for online. It will help you to find the demand for your products in the market. You can start a blog to share advantages and uses of your products. It will be a good platform to share information of new exciting offers and discounts.

Freelance Writing

As a freelance writer, you will get numerous exclusive opportunities to earn money. You can write a blog post, website content or a newsletter. If you are new to this field, make a strong portfolio. Before considering you for the post of freelance writing, the potential employers will like to check your writing style. For this purpose, you have to create samples by writing some blog posts. Post on different blogs as a guest to improve your writing skills. To find work, you can network with other freelance writers.

If you want to work as a freelance writer, you can get the advantage of numerous online platforms like Listverse. It is a good platform to earn online money. If you don't have prior experience as a writer, this can be a good platform for you to start your career. To work on this platform, you should have English writing and speaking qualities just like a native speaker, love for interesting and unusual things and sense of humor.

You have to write a list containing at least 10 items and send it to them. They will pay you $100 after checking your work, but make sure to have a PayPal account. If your work is not up to mark, they will say sorry and recommend you to improve your work.

3 Best ways to make more money with investing money

Starting an online business involves less risk than investing your money in a downtown or brick-and-mortar office. With your online business, you will get numerous chances to reach your potential customers and work from your home. To start a business setup, you will need communication skills and a well-designed website. If you have some maintenance know-how, you can manage your website in a better way. If you want to earn money with investing money, here are a few ideas for you.

Online Business

There are numerous highly profitable online businesses, such as fashion and clothing store, online classes or cookery shows. You can hire a professional designer to design a business website. On this website, you can offer your services or sell products. With e-commerce, you may initiate by partnering with different companies with useful products. If you can offer a discount on products, you can quickly win numerous customers and establish a strong ground for the store.

You can't do e-commerce business on a side because this business is really demanding and requires your maximum attention. It is unrealistic to expect immediate profits because you have to wait a while. E-commerce giants like Amazon also take some time to increase their profitability. Initially, you can focus on some growth strategies, such as digital marketing and guest blogging.

You can offer online training and consultancy as per your expertise in a particular field. It is a good idea to offer consultancy to all people in the world. Some good examples are bodybuilding classes, online accounting, finance advice classes, job placement, stock trading, coding classes, health and fitness, stock trading and cooking classes. You can design a website and promote your online business on your Facebook page.

Youtube Channel

Youtube is a famous platform to earn money. A Youtube channel will become your personal presence. Every Youtube account comes with an attached channel. It works similar to a Google account. After creating your Youtube account, you will be able to get access to numerous Google products like Drive and Gmail.

Create an account or utilize a current account and make sure to add keywords for the help of people to search your channel. It is essential to choose relevant keywords for your content. Your username may work against you. Choose a short and easy to recall username so that people can remember you. It is easy to change the username of your current Youtube account. A Youtube channel allows you to promote your products or services in a better way. Prepare demo videos for the use of your products or give online lectures. In short, you can earn a good amount of money with the use of a Youtube channel.

Affiliate Marketing

Affiliate marketing allows you to make a few bucks easily. An affiliate is someone who takes the commission for selling products of another company, whether on his/her own site or through an online channel, such as eBay. In this process, the best thing is that there is no need to develop a product yourself. You can sell products of other people. For instance, Amazon affiliates can reprobate in an obscene amount of commission in dollars. Just sign up to Amazon affiliate as an affiliate to sell the products of other people. You may use a referral link to sell these products. You will get a percentage of commission for every sold product without even lifting your finger.

The Commission may vary from product to product and may increase as per the number of sold products. The upper commission tier is almost 8%. It may add up to a serious amount of cash every month. You can increase your income by promoting products with the maximum commission. Affiliate networks, such as ClickBank or Sharesale offer a variety of products for promotion. Some highly contested niches are gambling and health. These niches can make you a millionaire. An online affiliate can earn a passive income for his/her family.

7 Steps to Write Your Very Own eBook for Kindle

If you want to write a successful eBook for publishing on Kindle, you can do this easily by following the following steps.

Find a good topic

The new eBook writers often make a mistake by picking an idea as per their own preferences. They don't bother to discover either this idea works in the market or not. Some topics may sound great, but these don't have a good market. There is no need to write a cookbook, self-help book or dieting book just because you consider it a good subject to earn money. If the market is saturated with certain books, then only established book and big names can earn a good profit.

If you have good knowledge about a topic, it will be better to select it to write an eBook. You will be able to enjoy writing on this subject. It will save your time and increase your chances of professional proofreading to the final draft of your book. Understand your purpose and mission to write a book. Create a list of possible ideas to write a book.

Research your topic

Market research is also important to look at the possible markets. You have to find out what is working and what subjects are not working. It won't take much time, but it will be fun to find out the work of other authors.

Regardless of your knowledge about a topic, you have to do good research on a topic. Make sure to check facts to offer interesting information to readers. Allocate sufficient time to research. Some writers find it easy to get stuck at the research stage to gather maximum sources and articles. They thumb through books and jot down references, facts, and quotes. You can avoid this situation by limiting your time for research. You can set 1 to 2 hours purely for your research before you start researching for a particular period.

Create chapters and outline

If you want to make writing easy, you have to write a clear outline before starting to write your book. Your outline must have the title of every chapter. Keep titles concise and interesting and it will be better to add 10 to 15 short chapters instead of writing 5 long chapters.
Subsections or subheadings in each chapter are necessary with a list of important information to cover in each subheading. A linear list or mind map can be a good choice to keep track of your work. You can get new ideas with this linear list and think strategically to link them.

Write 3 things for each chapter

Write down three things you want to talk about for each chapter. Make sure they are connected and that it is logical to write about them in the same chapter. You can use the information from your research and pick subjects to write about.

Write 500-1000 words for each chapter

People often get confused about the length of chapters. Keep them similar as much as possible and write 500 to 1000 words for each chapter. If you are unable to explain your point in the given limit, you can break this chapter to make 2 to 3 more chapters. Instead of writing lengthy chapters, you can break a topic to explain in more than 1 chapter.

Proofread your book

After writing your eBook, it is essential to proofread your book. You may find errors in your book and end up with more positive reviews. Proofreading can do lots of good for you book. It is even better to have 3 others proofread your book, so they can give you constructive feedback.

Come up with a title for your book

After editing your book, you are ready to move toward the title of your finished book. Selecting a title for your book is an important decision. Keep in mind that your title can increase or decrease the sale of your book. A book title is as important as a good headline of a newspaper. With a good title, people will more likely consider to read your book. You have to come up with the first and second title and both should be good enough to grab the attention of customers.

It will be good to choose descriptive titles instead of running after poetic titles. Simple language without esoteric words can easily grab the attention of readers. You can add some mystery in the book title, to make your title even more interesting.

One Last Thing…

If you enjoyed this book or found it useful I'd be very grateful if you'd post a short review on Amazon. Your support really does make a difference and I read all the reviews personally so I can get your feedback and make this book even better.

Thanks again for your support!

www.ingramcontent.com/pod-product-compliance
Lightning Source LLC
Chambersburg PA
CBHW050039230526
45470CB00003B/1357